Pony Ride

A Bananas in Pyjamas Story

by Richard Tulloch

an ABC BOOK

Rat in a Hat was setting up a riding school in the park.

He lent Amy a smart red riding jacket and a helmet.
'Come back later and your pony will be waiting,' said Rat.

Amy loved her new riding clothes.

'This afternoon Rat's going to give me riding lessons on a real pony!' said Amy.

The Bananas in Pyjamas were helping at Rat in a Hat's riding school.

They set up fences for the pony to jump over.
Rat's riding school was looking really good!

'Now where's the pony, Rat?' asked the Bananas in Pyjamas.
'Oh dear, I forgot to get a pony for the riding school!' said Rat.
Oh no, that Rat in a Hat!

'Are you thinking what I'm thinking, B1?'
'I think I am, B2.'
'It's Helping Time!'

The Bananas in Pyjamas thought they could help by dressing up as a pony for Rat's riding school.
B1 was the pony's front end.

And B2 was the pony's back end.

But the pony's front end went too fast ...

... and the pony's back end was left behind.

'I think I should be the head next time,' said B2.
'But I like being the head,' said B1.

The Bananas had a brilliant idea!

Later that day Amy arrived for her riding lesson.
She was very excited about riding on a real pony.

'This pony's name is Flash,' said Rat in a Hat proudly.

'I think Flash likes me,' said Amy, and she gave him a pat.

But when she climbed on to her pony ...

Amy got a big surprise!

'I thought Flash looked a bit Banana-ish,' she laughed.
'I'm sorry, Amy,' said Rat in a Hat. 'I knew you wanted to learn to ride but I forgot to get a pony.'

'Don't worry Rat,' said Amy. 'It was fun ...'
'And very funny too!' laughed Morgan, who arrived just in time to enjoy Amy's surprise.

And they all played pony races at Rat's riding school for the rest of the afternoon.